ROUTLEDGE LIBRARY EDITIONS:
PUBLIC ENTERPRISE AND
PRIVATIZATION

Volume 4

PUBLIC AND PRIVATE ENTERPRISE

PUBLIC AND PRIVATE ENTERPRISE

The Lindsay Memorial Lectures given at the University of Keele 1964

JOHN JEWKES

LONDON AND NEW YORK

First published in 1965 by Routledge & Kegan Paul Ltd

This edition first published in 2019
by Routledge
2 Park Square, Milton Park, Abingdon, Oxon OX14 4RN

and by Routledge
52 Vanderbilt Avenue, New York, NY 10017

Routledge is an imprint of the Taylor & Francis Group, an informa business

British Library Cataloguing in Publication Data
A catalogue record for this book is available from the British Library

ISBN: 978-0-367-14233-9 (Set)
ISBN: 978-0-429-25929-6 (Set) (ebk)
ISBN: 978-0-367-18164-2 (Volume 4) (hbk)
ISBN: 978-0-429-05990-2 (Volume 4) (ebk)

Publisher's Note
The publisher has gone to great lengths to ensure the quality of this reprint but points out that some imperfections in the original copies may be apparent.

Disclaimer
The publisher has made every effort to trace copyright holders and would welcome correspondence from those they have been unable to trace.

PUBLIC AND PRIVATE ENTERPRISE

The Lindsay Memorial Lectures

given at the University of Keele

1964

by

JOHN JEWKES

LONDON

ROUTLEDGE & KEGAN PAUL

First published 1965
by Routledge & Kegan Paul Ltd
Broadway House, 68–74 *Carter Lane*
*London, E.C.*4

Printed in Great Britain
by Latimer Trend & Co Ltd Plymouth

CONTENTS

LECTURE ONE

The State of the Debate

THE MAN in whose memory these lectures are delivered, Lord Lindsay of Birker, would, I think, have approved of the questions I intend to ask even though he might well not have agreed with some of my tentative answers. For Lindsay, as Professor Gallie has put it in his vivid little monograph,[1] held up the self-understanding society as the ideal, and in such a society high priority would have to be given to the understanding of the motives and forces which determine the respective roles of the individual and the State in economic life. Lindsay saw that the kind of society he preferred would demand intellectual leadership. He himself was, indeed, one such leader in his own day. Much that he concerned himself with has come to pass. He pleaded for more imagination in our thinking about education and especially about

[1] W. B. Gallie, *A New University: A. D. Lindsay and the Keele Experiment*.

university education. He saw the mass unemployment of the inter-war years as a great blot on our civilization. And, in other ways, time has caught up with the ideas for which he laboured so mightily.

The subject of my lectures is Public and Private Enterprise. Governments in the Western world are everywhere playing an increasingly important part in economic life. Everywhere, and not merely in Socialist countries, that part of the national income taken in taxation; of the working population employed by the State; of capital expenditure incurred by public authority, have all been on the increase over the past thirty or forty years. Recent important historical studies[1] have shown, for the United Kingdom, that public expenditure as a proportion of national income was relatively high in the nineteenth century up to about 1830, that it fell from 1830 to 1890 and thereafter started to increase again with the big changes coming after 1920. These broad statistics confirm the reports of acute observers of their times and reveal how the truisms of one era can well become the heresies of a later. Writing of the 1830's, De Tocqueville had this to say:[2]

[1] J. Veverka, 'The Growth of Government Expenditure in the United Kingdom since 1790'. *Scottish Journal of Political Economy*, vol. x, pp. 111–27.

[2] A. De Tocqueville, *Democracy in America*, World's Classics, pp. 566–7.

> Everywhere the State acquires more and more direct control over the humblest members of the community, and a more exclusive power of governing each of them in his smallest concerns. . . . Diversity, as well as freedom, are disappearing day by day. . . .

But after De Tocqueville came a change and, only forty years later, J. E. Cairnes was able to claim:[1]

> We are all now familiar with such commonplaces as that individuals are the best judges of their own interests; that monopolies should not be permitted in trade; that contracts should be free; that taxation should be equal; and should be directed towards the maintenance of the revenue and not to the guidance of commerce.

As late as 1926, Lord Keynes[2] could still speak of 'the strong bias in favour of *laissez-faire*' and of how 'State action to regulate the value of money, or the course of investment, or the population, provoke passionate suspicions in many upright breasts'. At least the first two of these are now accepted as functions of government.

It seems virtually certain that, unless there were a powerful reversal in social and political thinking, the growth of government activities will continue. In every Western country proposals are made for the

[1] J. E. Cairnes, 'Political Economy and *Laissez-Faire*' in *Essays in Political Economy, Theoretical and Applied*, 1873.

[2] J. M. Keynes, *The End of Laissez-Faire*, p. 15.

widening of welfare services, for controlling the location of industry, for more active public central economic planning. The most influential book on economics of the past decade, *The Affluent Society* by Professor Galbraith, is a plea for a large shift in favour of public as against private spending. Indeed, all paths seem to lead to wider government responsibilities. Rich countries, it is said, should expand public expenditure to prevent citizens from wasting their substance privately on trivialities. Poor countries must increase public investment, if necessary through forced savings, in order to induce more rapid economic growth. All countries must spend increasingly on publicly supported education and science because any one of them which falls behind will lose its place in the international economic league. All countries must increasingly provide free or heavily subsidized social services, and above all health services and housing, because these now cost so much that the ordinary man cannot possibly pay for his own needs. All big countries must, for safety, manufacture arms on a scale so massive that governments will be forced to take over, or at least dictate to, large sections of manufacturing industry. In industry generally, it is said, technology increasingly demands a scale of operation which surpasses the resources or the capacity for risk-taking of private institutions.

Before the Second World War it was frequently asserted by economic luminaries that the Western countries were passing into a phase of secular economic stagnation and the usual remedy proposed was a vast increase in public investment to fill the gap in aggregate demand. In our days it is just as frequently asserted that the Western world has entered into a period of dynamic change but, just the same, it is now recommended that government intervention is needed to stimulate science and technology even further, with the aim presumably of making dynamic conditions even more dynamic.

Now, it might be supposed that this impressive shift from private to public responsibility, with the prospects of more to come, could only have been brought about by the emergence of some new body of knowledge, some new line of reasoning which has made crystal clear to us the errors of our ways and has provided more rational guiding lines for the future.

In my opinion, this is not what has happened. Certainly, in Britain, whilst there has been vigorous, although often rambling, public discussions about specific cases, on the whole drift rather than systematic debate has determined the national course. Scholars in the social sciences seem to have been oddly unconcerned with what Edmund Burke described as

> One of the finest problems in legislation, namely to

> determine what the State ought to take upon itself to direct by the public wisdom and what it ought to leave, with as little interference as possible, to individual exertion.[1]

So that whilst these great changes have been going on, social scientists, and I think particularly economists, have been sitting on the sidelines.

When, indeed, they have intervened, it has not usually been in those ways in which scholars can claim authority. One might have expected to find them engaged in defining terms, examining the consistency between aims and methods, devising ways of measuring results, probing for the more complex reactions to policy, creating a picture of the whole from an analysis of the parts. For these things they have been trained and in these tasks they shine. On the contrary, in a mood almost of abnegation they have largely reconciled themselves to the idea that the main drift of the world will be determined by forces over which they have, and perhaps wish to have, no influence. So that the role of the economist is increasingly conceived of as that of helping governments to operate more efficiently, or less inefficiently, economic systems the general shape of which he is not prepared to examine critically.[2]

[1] Quoted by M'Culloch in his *Principles of Political Economy*.

[2] A forthright confession of this is to be found in R. L. Meek, 'Allocation of Expenditure in the Electricity Supply Industry',

All this is in sharp contrast to the attitudes and methods of earlier political economists. Whether, in fact, they arrived at the correct answers or not, Adam Smith, De Tocqueville, Hume, John Stuart Mill, Acton, Cairnes and other writers of their day set out to study their subject in the round in a manner which has rarely been matched in the literature of our own times. And where, as with Hayek's *Constitution of Liberty*, modern writers of great eminence have sought to fill the gap, their efforts have aroused much less interest than might have been expected.

One reason, I suppose, why social scientists have contracted out of the more ambitious role is that many, if not most of them, are happy at the shift towards increased public responsibility. Intellectuals as a whole seem strongly to dislike the market-place and all it implies.[1] Apart from that, it is not surprising that

in *Public Expenditure, Appraisal and Control*, edited by A. T. Peacock and D. J. Robertson. Mr. Meek says:

> The economists, too, are changing. They are increasingly leaving aside their role of critical observers of the economic system, and are being enlisted in large numbers to assist in the practical solution of certain basic problems of choice in large economic units (whether public or private) where the price mechanism can no longer be relied upon to solve them adequately. The economists are thus to an increasing extent assuming a role which had previously been associated more with war-time or the socialist economies.

[1] George J. Stigler, *The Intellectual and the Market Place.*

economists hesitate to raise fundamental issues and prefer to restrict themselves to efforts to make the world run a little more smoothly along a track which they feel that society, in some mysterious way, has already chosen for itself. For anyone who sets out to solve Burke's 'finest problem in legislation' is confronted by some daunting obstacles.

I turn to examine some of the most important of these.

The first is that every decision to expand or contract public economic activity has non-economic aspects. For example, if it were known that the nationalization of some British industry would make the country poorer, it might still be the right thing to nationalize if it could be established beyond doubt that the public attached overriding importance to the thought that, jointly and severally, they owned the assets of that industry. If it were accepted that the British National Health Service meant that the medical services available to the community were not, on the whole, as good as they might otherwise have been, the case for the Service might still be strong if the public set store by equality of treatment (of course, in practice, unattainable) and thought the Health Service was the best way of bringing this about.

The puzzle, of course, is how to strike the balance between the economic and the non-economic items.

In free societies it is done by engaging in prolonged and diffused discussions at every level: in newspapers and journals, through broadcasting, by public committees, by experts and those who are not so expert. Finally the issue is settled by debate and decision in Parliament. A decision thus arrived at is described as 'a political decision' and this rapidly becomes, especially for those who feel their views have prevailed, what is deemed to be 'a political fact'.

I am not quarrelling with this procedure. I can see no alternative to it. But if it embodies all the virtues of democracy, it also brings upon us most of its pains and penalties. In this case I cannot help but think that in much of such talk there is a bias: it lies in the fact that economic considerations get less than their proper weight and that faulty economic reasoning too often ousts sound.

This statement might, at first sight, seem surprising because, after all, economics is the most strongly established of the social sciences, its analytical methods have been highly developed and the historical and statistical material at its disposal is by now very extensive. Nevertheless, I believe it to be true.

In the making of public economic decisions there seems to be a propensity to underestimate costs and to exaggerate returns. In some extreme cases in recent years, costs and returns have even been regarded as the same thing—just as if a man who backed horses measured his winnings by adding up the total of the stakes that he had placed. For example, the case for increased expenditure on science as a way of increasing the national income has frequently been based on little more than the parading of figures of the enormous and constantly growing *expenditure* on scientific research. Again, the idea of opportunity cost—that the real cost of a thing is what one must do without in order to get that thing—is a very simple one. But it eludes or is evaded by very many people. Few of those who feel satisfied with a free public library system or a free health service ever bother to try to assess what they would do with the additional money they would have if these services were not publicly provided.

Of course, the principal reason why economic costs tend to be under-assessed is that, in communities where the distribution of income is unequal and where taxation on income is highly progressive, it comes to be widely thought that the majority of people are benefiting and that a small minority are meeting the costs. Recent studies,[1] however, show that in Great Britain the great majority of people pay for their own social services in taxation, rates and social insurance.

Again, politicians do not usually give us much help

[1] Arthur Seldon, *Rebirth of Britain*, p. 186.

in keeping economic costs in mind. It is no uncommon thing for governments, in the presentation of new schemes, to keep costs discreetly in the background or to present them at an optimistically low level or to dwarf their importance by assuming that they can be met out of some future hypothetical expansion of national income.

So that in the tumult which accompanies the balancing of the less tangible with the more tangible items, the standard warnings that 'you cannot have your cake and eat it' or 'you cannot get more than a pint out of a pint pot' or 'the community can always afford anything, anything so long as it gives up something else': all these tend to get pushed to one side and the economist may understandably weary of the odium which he calls down upon himself by drawing attention to these truisms.

The second snag in trying to solve Burke's problem is that of giving due weight to the broader overhead costs associated with the growth of government activities. It is a commonplace that every organization, as it increases in size, must face the danger that further growth will bring decreasing efficiency. For example, every large private business, as it gets bigger, struggles, and ultimately without effect, to resist the inertia of size. The burden of size has been the outstanding difficulty of the nationalized industries. I have no doubt that the same is true of universities, churches, armed forces and so on. The evil day can be put off but not for ever. Highly relevant illustrations of this point have been provided for us recently by the industrial mergers which have been so common in British industry. It is easy to understand how seductive these mergers can be. One profitable firm thinks that by absorbing another profitable firm it will make two profits instead of one. What is often left out of this calculation, and indeed is extremely difficult to calculate, is that the increased administrative burden thrown on the directors of the acquiring firm may stretch their powers to the point at which they perform their duties less adequately and the whole organization suffers in consequence.

This same factor ought clearly to be taken into account in deciding upon the claims for the extension of public enterprise. Cabinet Ministers, and even more so in the last resort a Prime Minister, have functions which only they can perform and which cannot be divided up or delegated. Any extension of government activity must throw heavier burdens upon them. No public enterprise will ever work so smoothly that nothing of importance will ever have to come to the centre where major decisions must finally be taken. So that whilst, superficially, it may seem that some new activity on the part of government has been successfully undertaken, it may be true that, in consequence, there has been a loss of effectiveness elsewhere. Because of the total pressure upon him of Cabinet affairs, a weary Foreign Secretary may miss a move in the search for peace, or a Chancellor of the Exchequer may be denied time to ponder over ways of improving methods of taxation or of preventing inflation. I wonder how many of the blunders made by politicians in our time have been made by men wearied beyond account or broken in health through prolonged overstrain.

One common rejoinder to all this is that governments can, in fact, widen their responsibilities greatly without getting bogged down in administration. I find this argument quite unconvincing and even dangerous. Thus it is claimed that a government may take responsibility for some new public service but take the whole operation 'out of politics' and thereby escape any increase in its own administrative burdens. For example, after 1945, it was sometimes argued that since each of the nationalized industries and services was to be placed under a Public Board and was not to be operated directly by a Department of State, swiftness of action in day-to-day affairs would be guaranteed and the burden thrown upon the Central Government would be limited to relatively infrequent decisions on matters of major policy. Experience in the past twenty years suggests that that view is naïve. Nationalization[1] has not taken industries out of the political arena. It has pushed them more firmly into it. So long as political parties are not agreed, some industries would seem to be in danger of being torn to pieces by constant switches between nationalization and denationalization. If nationalized industries are numerous, conflicts may and do arise between them which, if serious, may become matters of public concern and Ministerial intervention. Differences of opinion may arise between a Minister and those in charge of the Public Board and such differences inevitably become the subject of public debate. Cabinets will always be tempted to court popularity by giving way to democratic pressures for the provision of goods and services on exceptionally favourable terms or to uneconomic ends. To anyone who has watched what has happened to the Beeching Plan, the original suggestion that the operation of the railway system could be taken out of politics must represent one of the most artless propositions of all time.

It has proved impossible to give any real meaning to the distinction between matters of national interest or major policy on the one hand and matters of day-to-day importance on the other. The process of ad-

[1] On the whole subject of British Nationalization reference may be made to J. Jewkes, 'The Nationalization of Industry'. *University of Chicago Law Review*, Summer 1953.

ministration cannot be split up in this way. Wise policy on major matters can only be built up by careful scrutiny of day-to-day matters. No event, in the first instance, can be labelled as a minor or a major matter. The manner in which a minor event is dealt with may determine whether it becomes a major one in the operation of the organization. The very choice of what is a major and what is a minor matter (which function must surely be regarded as part of major policy) can only be exercised through day-to-day attention to what would normally be regarded as detail.

Again it is sometimes claimed that the span of government control can be widened without its grip becoming generally weaker by improving methods of what is called 'public accountability'. But no one has yet invented ways of doing this. In the early days of the nationalized industries many attempts were made to employ indices of physical efficiency for this purpose but these are clearly inadequate. They cannot present an overall picture. In effect, public accountability has taken the form of a series of grand inquests sometimes by Parliament, sometimes by outside bodies, which, in the last resort, have found themselves reaching qualitative conclusions through rough-and-ready judgments. And all this has involved much additional, hard, detailed work for Ministers at the highest level.

I make the simple point that even Ministers have

only twenty-four hours to the day and that any new work they take on may very well mean that they are forced to scamp their existing duties.

A third considerable obstacle in solving Burke's problem is that, even if it seemed otherwise desirable that the Government should undertake some new task, it may not be able to collect the necessary knowledge and develop the techniques to do what it sets out to do. When governments enlarge their functions they often do so by supplementing or replacing activities formerly carried through by the free market. Now public enterprise relies to a much greater degree than private upon statistics and measurement as instruments of control. This distinction is partly a matter of scale; a small manufacturer knows from long experience the details of his own business and will depend to a lesser degree upon figures than a government department which is operating a national industry and has to determine proper scales of output and correct regional and local distributions and so on. It is partly a matter of the form of the institution; a business man in a competitive market does not have to think a great deal about price, that is fixed for him by competition, but a government monopolist can fix prices within limits and presumably must determine those prices after national studies of demand and supply. And it is partly a matter of difference of function; thus a government for its full employment policy must collect for its own special purposes statistics of national income and related quantities.

Can these economic measurements be made with sufficient accuracy and speed for government purposes? Are they such useful instruments for the devising of sound policy as is often claimed? I think that some of the inherent limitations of statistics are too often overlooked.

Some eminent statisticians have for long been warning us of the rickety statistical structures upon which much economic reasoning in these days is based. Quite recently, Professor Morgenstern[1] has left us in no doubt as to the perils we run. He shows that even with American and British figures, which are perhaps the best in the world, critical statistics are being relied upon which have very wide margins of error. He asserts that

> National income and consumers' spending power probably cannot be known now in part without an error of ±10 to ±15 per cent.

With the accepted margins of error in the figures out of which the British National Income statistics were drawn up, the variation in Gross Domestic Capital Formation between 1954 and 1955 could have been as low as minus £37 million or as high as plus £1,119

[1] Oskar Morgenstern, *On the Accuracy of Economic Observations*.

million. Other almost equally striking ranges of possible error might be quoted. Mistakes in British government policy due to errors in the best available balance of payments statistics have been common in the past fifteen years.

So that Ministers may be organizing changes which lie within the margin of error of the statistics they are using. They may be relying upon a recorded trend just the opposite of what is actually occurring. The crucial point here is that some of the weaknesses in the relevant information are inevitably bound up with that kind of knowledge. There is a constant demand for more comprehensive statistics more promptly collected and published; but, in the nature of things, the more quickly the statistics are collected and published, the wider the likely margins of error. This is not merely a matter of preparing 'an up-to-date Bradshaw', to use the language once employed by Mr. Macmillan, by which he revealed that he was really missing the point. It is far more subtle and serious than that. It is a matter of governments crying for the moon; embarking upon courses which, if they are to be rationally pursued, call for more and more accurate knowledge than can be collected.

One error fostered by overconfidence in the accuracy of economic statistics is the belief that the economic future can be predicted. That way lies nothing but disenchantment. For if it were true that the economic future could be foreseen, there would be no reason for doubting the possibility of predicting the future in all its other aspects and hence of knowing the whole course of future world events. The odd thing is that economic soothsayers often believe that their long-term forecasts have greater reliability than their short; the further they are asked to probe into the future, the more confident they appear to feel that they can produce the right answer. Perhaps the fact that the day of reckoning, in these cases, is farther off has something to do with this attitude.

The inescapable uncertainties of the future seem to me to be one of the critical determinants of what governments should try to do and what success they are likely to have. The more striking errors in economic prediction in the past have not, I think, been sufficiently studied. If they had, they might have made us much wiser about the value of peering into the future. Some prognostications, indeed, have changed the course of history; such as Karl Marx's prediction of the inevitable deterioration in the standard of living of the working classes under capitalism or Engel's that by the middle of the twentieth century the gulf between richer and poorer in England would have become wider and deeper and that child labour would always be an essential feature of modern industrialization.[1] But some of the less spectacular cases have a good deal to teach us. Writing in the 1830's, De Tocqueville, in his *Democracy in America*,[2] confidently predicted that the United States would become the greatest shipbuilding and shipping country in the world. Yet it is in exactly those two directions that the American industrial system, so powerful otherwise, has proved extraordinarily feeble. This case is significant because De Tocqueville arrived at his erroneous conclusions after the most careful and cautious analysis of past events (indeed his methods would be a model for some of our latter-day exponents of extrapolation) and even more so because his error in economic matters contrasts so sharply with the breath-taking accuracy with which he examined American political institutions and deduced from this analysis the kind of nation and people which would emerge. Perhaps reliable prediction in the political field is easier than in the economic!

I am not, of course, claiming that economic prediction is always incorrect; if this were true there would be at least one way of knowing for certain what would not happen. But let me remind you that in Great Britain in the late 1920's, alarming forecasts were

[1] Engels, *Condition of the Working Classes in England*. Edited by W. O. Henderson and W. H. Chaloner, p. xvi.

[2] Vol. I. New Edition, 1875, pp. 431–9.

being made in well-respected quarters about the future size of the population. Phrases such as 'race suicide' were not thought too extreme to apply to the prospects for the rest of this century. The opposite of all this has proved to be true and it is sometimes now suggested that our increasing population constitutes one of our economic burdens. These pre-war forecasts darkened counsel in many ways.

It is sometimes assumed that so many errors of prediction have been made in the past that the experts will be less likely to make such mistakes in the future. I see no grounds for that optimistic assumption. Not merely because history rarely repeats itself and, if it does, there is no way of knowing when such a rare occurrence is impending. But also because it seems that in the modern world the variable factors are more numerous than they used to be. I will, therefore, draw my third illustration from very recent events. For long, experts seem to have been guilty of misjudging the future supply of sources of energy[1] and governments, in consequence, have been led into ill-starred action. In 1956 a Committee of the Organization for European Economic Co-operation, in its Report, *Europe's Growing Needs of Energy*, produced a most disturbing picture of what was described as 'the gap' between the

[1] G. Tugendhat, *Freedom for Fuel.* Institute of Economic Affairs, 1963.

consumption of energy in Europe and its indigenous production. The Committee heavily discounted the chance that imports, especially from the Middle East, could fill this gap; they went on to recommend urgent action to develop home production of energy, particularly by increasing the output of coal. The forecasting of this Committee could hardly have been wider of the mark. I think that its findings contributed to overprecipitate action on the part of Great Britain in planning for the production of power through the use of atomic energy. Some four years later another Committee of O.E.E.C., in its Report, *Towards a New Energy Pattern in Europe*, corrected the errors of the earlier one. But even this second Committee seems to have missed the deeper significance of the incident. It comments:

> We believe that the dangers of such forecasting [needed for immediate decisions on long-term investments] are minimized . . . if such forecasts are constantly subject to revision and if every effort is made to hold the balance between the inevitable moods of excessive optimism and pessimism which may particularly affect these long projections.

But what is the significance of a forecast when it is constantly subject to revision? And where are to be found those supermen, insulated against all the human emotions, who will instinctively recognize excessive optimism or pessimism when they see it and have such a gift of tongues that they will be able to convince the rest of us of our mistakes before it is too late?

But to return to the main line of the argument.

Those who conclude that the quest for a way of organizing society which makes sense economically is not worth the effort may do so for one of several reasons. Some say that economic issues should take a back seat anyway; that the things that matter are national independence and prestige, justice, equality; that being a little richer or poorer is very much a secondary issue. Some that more or less public intervention does not, in any case, affect the efficiency of the economic system significantly, that countries which have drawn the line at very different places show roughly similar standards of living. Some that, whilst the extent of public intervention possibly does make a difference, since we cannot determine the difference scientifically, it is better not to set out on a task which cannot be performed well. And some, who tell us that the problem of production is solved, feel that there can be little value in efforts which will simply increase the promised forthcoming surfeit of goods. In brief, these groups all argue that Burke was wrong, that this is not one of the finest problems of legislation but is in fact one potentially unrewarding.

I confess that I am less negative in my attitude than

that. I know it is common for some poorer countries officially to declare that national independence and the satisfaction of running their economic affairs in their own way are aims for which they are prepared if necessary to make any economic sacrifice. Yet these countries are usually the first to point out the moral obligation of others to provide economic help and the first to warn that if their standards of living do not rise then serious political and social consequences will follow. In brief, like the rest of us, they would prefer to give everything top priority. I know, too, it is fashionable in the richer Western countries to maintain that, with their present levels of affluence, the little more or less should not cause anxiety. Yet in each one of these countries there appears to be a constant dread of falling behind in the race with the international Jones's. Indeed, far from this being the age in which economic matters are philosophically put out of mind, it might better be described as the age of the New Materialism.

Again, I do not see great force in the argument that economic institutions do not matter, that they have little influence upon standards of living. In the extreme case, this statement is clearly unproved. For centuries men have been dreaming of economic communities so scientifically organized from the centre that any predetermined level of living could be attained. Yet, despite numerous attempts to realize these ambitions (to take a special case, despite fifty years in Russia of an experiment in which individual rights have never been allowed to stand in the way of national economic aims) it is still true that the rich countries in the world are those which have accepted certain types of economic institutions and the poorer countries those which have not accepted them. If this be true as between the extremes, may it not be true, to a lesser degree, within the extremes?

I further contend that the economist does possess knowledge and, by training and experience, should be able to acquire a know-how which gives him the right to discuss the main features of an economic society and should not resign himself to act as a hewer of wood and a drawer of water in a society built to the specifications of others. Keynes,[1] in one of his lighter essays, once urged us not to take economic problems too seriously. He looked to the day when economics would be a matter for specialists. And he went on:

> If economists could manage to get themselves thought of as humble, competent people on a level with dentists, that would be splendid!

Society has benefited enormously from the fact that he did not impose upon himself any such self-denying ordinance.

[1] J. M. Keynes, *Essays in Persuasion*, p. 373.

And, despite anything I have already said, we can congratulate ourselves on the fact that public thinking on weighty and complex economic subjects is becoming more sophisticated. There is wider acceptance of the truism that a government has nothing to distribute save what it first collects from the community. There is a cooler and more sceptical approach in these days to the claims that big organizations are necessarily more efficient than smaller. It is not wholly chimerical to imagine that societies can examine soberly what economic institutions conform best to their economic hopes.

LECTURE TWO

Some Special Cases

In my first lecture I suggested that we ought not to neglect the broader consequences of the changing balance between public and private enterprise. As the poet Roy Campbell once wrote:

> Things have a nearer meaning to their looks,
> Than to their dead analysis in parts.

But we clearly cannot ignore the lessons to be drawn from the case-by-case method. The pragmatic approach was not overlooked by the main liberal writers, all of whom were prepared to regard favourably as proper functions of the State those which passed the following tests:

1. Where a given expenditure would bring an even larger economic return to the community but would not be undertaken by any private individual.

2. Where a given expenditure, although not necessarily yielding an economic return in the narrow sense,

could nevertheless be shown to be 'really important to the general interest'.

3. Where the individual in striving, in apparently rational fashion, for some benefit or the avoidance of some harm, would normally be led to take action which would frustrate his own purposes.

4. Where it could be shown that the State, for one reason or another, would be able to produce goods or services more cheaply than private enterprise.

Applying these tests, there is much common ground as to what are the legitimate functions of the State. Defence, justice, law and order, a high and stable level of employment, town and country planning, the care of the needy, taxation and currency would be at the top of the list. (Note, however, that most Governments in recent years have neglected their responsibility for improving methods of taxation and for preserving the value of the currency.) The next group includes important services for which prices cannot normally be charged: preventive medicine, some branches of education and research, information, flood control, drainage and land recovery. In a third group the advantages of central co-ordination may call for State responsibility: postal services, telephones, and perhaps the supply of gas, water and electricity.

It is, however, in the study of those cases about which people do not agree that we get to grips seriously

with the subject. In Great Britain in recent years the major and most complex *topics* have been nationalization of industry or of such services as health and broadcasting; the public support of science, technology and education generally; the control of the location of industry and the conservation of natural resources, especially of land. These topics raise, in varying admixtures, the same important *issues*: what economies are to be gained from operating on the largest possible scale; what advantages flow from monopoly operation; and what criteria should determine the degree to which public should supplement, where it is not intended to supplant, private effort.

One might discuss the topics in terms of the issues or the issues in terms of the topics but I propose to follow the latter course and I turn first to the question of the optimum size of operation.

The defence of State economic activity on the score that a government will normally operate on a larger scale than a private individual or institution and therefore will be likely to produce goods and services at a lower cost is found fairly widely, but it has been advanced with greatest confidence in relation to the nationalization of industry and it can therefore be most usefully examined in that connection.

At first sight it seems an odd idea that the whole of an industry that happens to fall within one national

boundary should be regarded as the most efficient unit for production. Optimum size would seem to be a function of technical and marketing conditions, of the normal rate of innovation and so on. These would seem to have little or no relation to the historical accidents which have determined the boundaries of one country. Certainly this proved to be the case with the British nationalized industries. For no sooner had they begun to operate than it became clear that, far from their size being a virtue, it constituted their most persistent and troublesome problem. This even the most ardent advocates of nationalization have pointed out. As one of them put it:[1]

> Some of the administrative problems of the nationalized industries arise from the very size of the industries taken over. Bigness is perhaps their greatest drawback.

It has proved, indeed, a drawback difficult to overcome. This accounts for the long string of public and private inquiries into the working of these Public Boards. The reports of the investigating committees have see-sawed between the view that more de-centralization was needed in order to inject life and a local sense of responsibility into the organization and the opposite view that less de-centralization was de-

[1] Ernest Davies, *Problems of Public Ownership*. Labour Party Pamphlet, 1952.

sirable, that tighter centralization was called for in order to transmit through the organization the superior wisdom and knowledge thought to reside at the centre. Usually what was recommended by one committee was the opposite of what had last been tried, but without benefit, as the result of the recommendations of an earlier committee. The other side of the road has always seemed to be less muddy. These fluctuating views should not be a matter of surprise. They flow from the fact that the various committees were trying to deal with what may well have been an insoluble problem. The nationalized industries were so large as to make it dubious whether they could *ever* be efficiently operated, whether they had not outstripped the limits of administrative feasibility. This has never been admitted explicitly. But implicitly it has been accepted by the action of both political parties: even the Labour Party has devoted much thought to other possible forms of public ownership which would place upon the Government much more restricted responsibilities as to the detail in which and the scale upon which the Government would take charge of an industry.

I think there are two simple lessons to be drawn from the history of nationalization. The first is that industries, and particularly the newer ones, present us with diversity and intricacy too great to be conceived of except by those who have to try to deal with

them. The National Coal Board, in trying to make a full list of its assets, in an industry commonly regarded as homogeneous, once rather wistfully confessed:

> It was a process like the making of the Doomsday Book.

The second moral is that increasing size is not a cure-all for the troubles of any institution, it may be a positive menace. And this point is just as relevant in public policy relating to mergers in private industry as it is in the matter of nationalization.

What are claimed as the special virtues of monopoly when it is vested in public hands? (Note that the claim that a government should prohibit all private persons from doing certain things is the very opposite of the more common one that the government should step in only where the individual cannot or will not act.)

The reasons put forward for public monopoly have been numerous and varied. Sometimes they have been technical. Thus it has been said that if coalmining is placed under one national authority then coal reserves can be exploited more systematically, without obstruction from individual land or mineral rights. But coal does get mined quite efficiently in countries which do not have this form of centralized public control. In the generation and distribution of electricity, central control makes it possible to bring a balance between deficits and surpluses in different regions; although the

same effect might be achieved by special agreements between otherwise independent generators. The British Broadcasting Corporation has argued for monopoly on technical grounds because of the limited number of wavelengths available. But in their joint evidence before the Broadcasting Committee in 1949,[1] Sir Robert Watson-Watt and Sir Geoffrey Crowther rejected the argument and what has happened since suggests that they were right.

Sometimes the case for a publicly operated or conferred monopoly is submitted on grounds of welfare. It used to be argued that the monopoly powers vested in the nationalized industries gave them the chance of supplying privileged or needy groups at exceptionally low prices. This argument is much less frequently met with now. Sometimes monopoly is recommended because it can be used to raise cultural or moral standards. Lord Reith, in his unswerving advocacy of what he usually referred to as 'brute monopoly in broadcasting', based his argument mainly upon 'the paramount importance of the preservation of a high moral tone' in the community. And when he was in a position to determine these things, he went into detail as to how this should be interpreted. He had particularly austere views about what we should be allowed to listen to on

[1] Report of the Broadcasting Committee, 1949. Appendix H, pp. 333–41.

the Sabbath.[1] But, as the recent popularity of broadcasting from pirate radio ships has made clear, the efforts, however lofty, of one individual or group to improve the standards of another simply by restricting their range of choice, can have powerful boomerang effects.

There is another much more important, interesting and at first glance cogent defence of monopoly. It can be presented as the condition precedent to order and rationality in the economic system. It appeals to many as the obvious way of bringing about what is variously described as integration or co-ordination or unification. Behind this is the tacit assumption that order in the economic system cannot exist unless it is consciously engineered by one or a small group of men. It constitutes a denial that there can be such a thing as spontaneous order.

This anxiety about what might go wrong unless there is constant and conscious guidance in the economic system can best be illustrated by reference to transport. There are different forms of transport and it seems sensible that each should be devoted to the purpose which it best serves. Everyday observation appears to indicate that there is much duplication. Vehicles are seen to be travelling in the same direction

[1] R. H. Coase, *British Broadcasting: A Study in Monopoly*, Chapter III.

only partly full. Road, rail, air and water facilities exist on the same routes. Surely, it can be argued, if one organization could only get all the pieces of this jigsaw puzzle under its control, vast savings would be possible.

Thus when the British Transport Commission was first set up in 1947 it began with the widest possible interpretation of this idea:

> Rail, road and inland water services were to be developed as complementary to each other and were not to be regarded as rival forms of transport.[1]

Yet, over the years, the seductive concept of a waste-free fitting together of these different services has proved a will-o'-the-wisp. There is no such thing as 'transport' in the sense in which the Commission at first envisaged it. There is only the individual consumer who, for one reason or another which is good to him, will prefer to travel between two points by one method of transport rather than another. Or there is the individual manufacturer, who for one of a thousand reasons may prefer to have his goods carried in one way rather than another. Anyone trying to solve this jigsaw puzzle is confronted with an infinite number of possible permutations of preferences by consumers, in

[1] 'Statement of Policy on the Integration of Freight Services By Road and Rail.'

the face of which the would-be integrator does not really know where to start.

This is exactly what has happened in the case of the early ambitions of the British Transport Commission. Gradually it has been forced back, in its search for some practicable basis for action, to virtually the opposite ideas from which it started. In its 1950 Report it is found saying:

> The Commission had no intention of operating integration schemes which would impair freedom of choice where regular services of different kinds are available between the same points.

And in its 1951 Report it moved further:

> All the Commission ask is that the customer shall pay the real cost of the service he selects and that he shall not receive one service at its bare cost if he insists at the same time on the maintenance of other services at less than cost.

On the whole, perhaps, these simple lessons are being accepted. The view is now widely held that prices and costs should be closely related, not merely in order to enable nationalized industries to shed their special welfare responsibilities but also to bring about a more economical use of resources with closer conformity to the preferences of the consumer. But this is largely an abandonment of the argument in support of monopoly.

The three most widely discussed cases where the State may supplement (sometimes of course on a very extensive scale) private effort are education, scientific research and health services. All these may afford, to the individual, consumer benefits which have nothing to do with his power to produce. I am concerned here only with the latter. If increased expenditure makes individuals more efficient or creates an environment conducive to economic growth, we ought to be able to explain how this happens and how far the benefits extend. I fear that I shall have time only to examine the subject of education from this angle, but I shall make bold to absorb into my conclusions the inquiries I have conducted in other fields.[1] I would like to be quite sure here that I am not being mistaken. I happen to be in favour of more higher education for its own sake. I hope that much more imagination will be shown in experiments with new ways of educating, new sizes and types of educational institutions, different ways of financing education. I am so much in favour of all these that I would not wish people to be deterred from

[1] J. & S. Jewkes, *Value for Money in Medicine. Blackwell*, 1963. J. Jewkes, 'How Much Science?'. *Economic Journal*, March 1960.

making sacrifices in other directions in order to be able to pay for their own education if they cannot otherwise get what they want. But here I am dealing with something else. I am concerned with whether a strictly economic case can be made out for more education and for how much more.

It has recently been propounded, almost as if in the nature of a new discovery, that education, 'investment in human capital' is, after all, the most powerful force making for economic progress. Actually the classical economists discussed the same subject in almost the same terms but, to my mind, with greater discrimination and subtlety. But modern writers have put their conclusions into arresting quantitative terms. One, for example, claims that in the United States between 1929 and 1957 education could be credited with 42 per cent of the increase in the real national income per person employed.[1] Clearly, if economic returns to additional education in the future are likely to be anything of this order, we cannot afford not to have a lot more of it.

Why this sudden resurgence of interest in education? It seems to have emerged almost as a side consequence of the fashionable belief that 'economic progress is not an autonomous historical process that hap-

[1] E. Denison, *The Sources of Economic Growth in the United States*. See also T. W. Schultz, *The Economic Value of Education*, p. 11.

pens accidentally but an evolution which can be promoted by deliberate action and planning'.[1] But what should this deliberate action and planning be? The search for a theoretical answer and for practical steps for giving effect to it have led to some artless thinking and some costly errors. The first false start was to assume that the secret through which governments could induce economic growth was to invest more and more. Experience, however, revealed that, even in Western countries, there was no obvious correlation between the supply of capital and economic expansion and that, in underdeveloped countries, great waste followed from attempts to put the doctrine into effect. Nevertheless, the delusion has persisted that somewhere there is a simple key to the opening of Pandora's Box. The emphasis has now swung round to science and even more so to education as the answers to the search.

Since something must have been responsible for economic growth in Western countries in recent years, that part of it which could not be explained by reference to the most obvious factors has come to be attributed to education as the 'residual' element. But the residual element tends to be inordinately large because it is really a measure of our ignorance of all the

[1] *Science, Economic Growth and Government Policy*. Organization for Economic Co-operation and Development, 1963, p. 9.

numerous and intricate forces which determine economic growth. Those who do not subscribe wholeheartedly to the current popular fashion of thought and believe that economic progress *is*, in large measure, an autonomous historical process, would stress that economic growth is much more than a matter of the quantities of land, capital, labour, science, education and so on which are mixed together in the economic system but of the manner in which they are so mixed. Here one would also have to take into account everything included within another blanket term 'enterprise': the will to get things done, to take the initiative, to organize, to build, to possess material things, to exercise economic power, and also the incentives which exist for generating these driving forces. Here we have, to use the language of the moment, 'parameters of action' which students of economic growth will find awkward to measure but which can be neglected only at the cost of departing from reality.

Let us now turn to the narrower, more formal statistical exercises by which the importance of education as a factor in economic growth has been assessed.

The line of reasoning runs thus:

> People who have enjoyed a higher education on the average earn more than others. When the additional cost of this higher education is set against the subsequent larger income, the rate of return for the individual

on his investment is high as compared with rates of return in other directions. So it would presumably pay other individuals to make similar investment in better education for themselves. But in addition to these private advantages there are social economic advantages flowing from a general improvement in education. So there are good reasons why public expenditure, as a replacement of or a supplement to private expenditure, is desirable.

The links in this chain of argument are slender for more than one reason.

1. A person who is trained as a doctor instead of becoming, say, a carpenter will presumably show higher earnings in consequence. But if many more doctors were trained, the earnings of doctors themselves, including the existing doctors, would fall. It is conceivable that the total earnings of all doctors might decrease. Would the rate of return on investment in education then be considered negative?

2. If those who have had the higher education are in fact a special group, perhaps more intelligent or enterprising than the average, they might well have earned higher than average incomes even without their superior education. What would the figures mean then?

3. The cost of education does not consist wholly of the cost of teachers, schools and equipment. There is also the cost in the form of production lost when

people are at school or university and therefore not producing in industry or commerce. This element is surprisingly large; it has been estimated as amounting to more than one-half of the cost of higher education in the United States.[1] Any further extension of higher education would clearly impose progressively higher costs in the form of foregone production.

There are some broader doubts which might be felt about any straight-line connection between the scale of education and the rate of economic growth.

Might not the rapid extension of higher education, as that term is now understood, reduce rather than increase economic production?

Education can be provided so inefficiently that it defeats its own objects and then better education would follow from a reduction of expenditure. James Mill refused to send his children to school 'lest the habit of work should be broken and a taste for idleness acquired'. Dr. Arnold once protested that

> I would far rather send a boy to Van Dieman's Land where he must work for his bread than send him to Oxford to live in luxury without any desire in his mind to avail himself of his advantages.

Professor Machlup has recently argued with force that education in the United States could probably be im-

[1] F. Machlup, *The Production and Distribution of Knowledge in the United States*, p. 105.

proved and at the same time be made cheaper by cutting down the period reserved for education and expecting children to work harder at school.[1] Perhaps not enough attention is paid to all this at present.

There are even more important points. Education does not only equip us to do more effectively the things we want to do. It influences us as to what is worth while doing, producing and enjoying. In the words of Francis Bacon:

> Knowledge is not a shop for profit or sale, but a rich storehouse for the glory of the Creator and the relief of man's estate.

Samuel Smiles, who if living today might well be shocked at the narrow commercial conception of the value of education as revealed in the writings of some modern welfare economists, had this to say on the subject:[2]

> To regard self-culture . . . as a means of getting past others in the world . . . rather than as a power to elevate the character and expand the spiritual nature, is to place it on a very low level.

Education, that is to say, may change the social targets to the detriment of physical productivity. John Stuart Mill put it thus:[3]

[1] Op. cit., p. 136.
[2] Samuel Smiles, *Self Help*. Edition of 1907, p. 390.
[3] *Principles of Political Economy*. New Edition, 1909, p. 106.

> Every real improvement in the character of the English, whether it consist in giving them higher aspirations, or only a juster estimate of the value of their objects of desire, must necessarily moderate the ardour of their devotion to the pursuit of wealth.

Education which is directed towards practical results may miss the mark. Even in science, for hundreds of years the teaching of alchemy was pure misdirection of effort. The history of medicine suggests that, apart from preventive medicine, until recently medical education had been of little practical value. I myself would doubt the value of a great deal of recent economic teaching about short-cuts to material prosperity, and indeed much of this has already been discarded. So soon as education comes to be regarded as a prime instrument in hastening economic growth the sharpest differences of opinion emerge as to what sort of education should enjoy the highest priority, with the advocates of one form of education branding another form as useless or wasteful. Scientists begin to decry the value of education in the humanities. Thus the late Lord Cherwell:[1]

[1] Speaking in the House of Lords, 21st November 1956. Sir Alexander (now Lord) Todd also is reported as saying: To suggest that more than a modest number of those now studying, say, history or literature in our universities were being trained to the best advantage was not only nonsense but at the present time dangerous nonsense.

(*The Times*, 3rd January 1957)

> Humanistic studies are agreeable, and were very valuable in their day. But they do not really help the country to survive today. . . . The fact remains that the people of this country must be fed and clothed. . . . The contribution of a man like Whittle was even more helpful to the people of this country than the efforts of any of the Regius Professors of History in our own universities.

Again, there are those who would be prepared to check science in the interests of technology in our Universities.[1]

Every new twist and turn in fashionable ideas about what is retarding economic growth seems to go along with a recommendation that a higher proportion of our able young people should be trained in one direction or another. If State economic planning breaks down, then it is argued that more people must be educated in economics and statistics. If management appears to be failing, then the demand is for more Schools of Management in the Universities. If our export products are thought to fail in industrial design, then it is argued

[1] Thus Lord Bowden, Minister of State for Education and Science, after claiming that the countries doing best in the economic race were those that put the emphasis on applied research went on 'this was going to be the extraordinarily difficult and agonizing reappraisal—how far could one allow the best brains to be diverted into subjects where immediate impact on the economy was not sufficiently obvious'. (*The Times*, 3rd December 1964)

that more young people should be drafted into Arts Schools. If it is thought that our exports flag because our salesmen do not frequently enough speak the language of the foreigner, then more people should be drafted into the Language Schools of Universities. These conflicting voices cannot all be correct. They may, indeed, all be misleading. For they tend to drive out of the curricula those broad subjects of study which no one can defend as having direct relevance for economic expansion but which contribute much to general intelligence and the instinct for orderly living without which economic achievement would be inconceivable. Again, whilst very many different disciplines can be employed as the instruments for educating the young successfully, each individual is a law unto himself. If more education is attempted through the teaching of subjects for which the individual may have no natural affinity or sympathy but which accord best, in the minds of authority, with plans for economic expansion, then more education will be carried on against the grain of the individual and render the labours of the teacher progressively less rewarding.

In thinking of the connection between more education and increased output it is sometimes more exact to think of them not as cause and effect but much more as effect and cause. To take a simple illustration: if a way is found of increasing the speed of a machine and thereby its physical output, it may be that this is only feasible if more lubricating oil is fed to the machine to offset the growing friction. This does not mean that the larger supply of oil is a *cause* of the increased output; it does not mean that further increases in output will follow from even heavier lubrication. The additional quantity of oil needed is a cost and it might conceivably be so high that it proves not to be worth while to speed up the machine. So, too, at times with education. Adam Smith pointed out that the division of labour would increase output but was also likely to destroy the intrinsic interest in work and make men narrow-minded and that more education was needed to counter the effects of these undesirable reactions.[1] The principle of specialization is applied in our days to more and more activities; hence the popular complaint that gaps are appearing between the different 'cultures', that too many men are being given the ill-balanced training which produces lop-sided characters. If more general education is recommended to offset this, it will be an additional cost to be set against the immediate economic benefits of specialization.

Experience suggests that growth in the past can partly be attributed to personal efforts and qualities of

[1] E. G. West, 'The Role of Education in Nineteenth Century Doctrines of Political Economy'. *British Journal of Educational Studies*, May 1964.

a kind which are not specially fostered within the academic halls. In making the tally of the forces responsible for economic growth in the Western world in the past two or three decades, to go back no earlier, we cannot leave out of account the contributions of a limited number of outstanding industrial entrepreneurs. Most of these men have absorbed themselves in tasks calling for much action of no great or varied intellectual interest; they have been willing and have possessed the nervous energy to take risks; they have possessed the sanguine outlook which enables a man to reach a policy decision even when a good deal of information theoretically necessary is not available. I would doubt whether their success can be attributed to formal education or whether wider formal education would have produced more men of the same kind.

To put this point more generally: this is an age of specialization and in so far as we are concerned with getting economic results, specialization in the preparation for life has to be accepted. Specialization consists of directing the attentions of the individual to a few only of all the forms of knowledge and skill and diverting his interest from other forms. I think, for instance, that healthy academic life, the pursuit of truth, vitally depends upon some members and groups in society remaining comparatively indifferent to money making. I think, conversely, that economic expansion will depend upon the presence of other groups with peculiar capacities and acumen who may have what others may deem an over-regard for money making. And this will not be fostered by higher education as we now understand it.

There is also the big and largely unplumbed question of the relation between education and original and inventive thinking. University education, even at its best, tends to bring about conformist thinking; for Universities cannot operate without standard tests and procedures. Might this have the effect of raising the average level of competence but only at the expense of frustrating the rarer spirits? It certainly seems true that if one takes the men who have broken through the existing barriers in the arts, in science and technology, a significant proportion of them would have been, or were, frustrated by the minimum degree of organization called for if we are to have formal higher education at all. Perhaps the answer here is that more higher education should not mean simply exposing more young people to the accepted present routine of academic life but should include other ways of providing leisure and resources by which the young can learn in their own ways and pursue their eccentricities.

Taking all these things into account I can understand, and have great sympathy with, Sir Sydney Caine who, in a recent article examining the grounds upon which the rapid extension of our present University system was being advocated, commented[1]

> The level of discussion must be intensely depressing to any believer in scientific method.

It would, indeed, be paradoxical if we were to accept as good arguments for a rapid extension of higher education the flabby kind of reasoning which good education is supposed to eradicate.

As with education, so with science and health services. Very large increases have been made in the expenditure on science and on research and development since the end of the Second World War and most people believe that this has brought great economic returns. This may or may not be true. But there is no straightforward confirmation of it. The things that might have been expected to happen if it were correct have not always happened. For instance, as between different countries, it does not seem to be true that the countries which, proportionately, have spent most on research and development show the most rapid industrial expansion. The opposite is more nearly true. America and Great Britain seem to have been the heaviest spenders proportionately on research but those are the two countries where it is most frequently

[1] Sir Sydney Caine, 'Education as a Factor of Production.' *Lloyds Bank Review*, April 1964.

complained that industrial output has lagged behind in the international race. On the other hand, Japan, which shows the most impressive rate of economic growth in recent years has not engaged in research and development on any extraordinary scale. If we take the United States alone, where the statistics are most complete and where research expenditure has reached astronomical levels, the annual percentage rate of growth in industrial production is not higher than it was half a century ago. The number of patents taken out in that country have not been increasing. Some American writers, in an attempt to show a positive correlation, have been driven to compare expenditure on research with the actual number of scientific papers published—which seems to me to make something of a mockery of the whole subject. In Great Britain the Zuckerman Committee[1] once, somewhat rashly, assumed a simple 1-for-1 correspondence between the number of scientific and technical workers and industrial output; but it quickly had to drop this assumption in the light of experience.

As for the National Health Service, it has often been argued, and was especially so at the time of its inauguration, that more money spent on medicine in this

[1] *Scientific and Engineering Manpower in Great Britain.* Office of the Lord President of the Council and the Ministry of Labour and National Service, 1956.

way would bring an economic return in the form of less absenteeism through sickness, greater working efficiency and a longer working life following from increased longevity. But sickness absence rates do not seem to be on the decline in Western countries and the effect of increased longevity on the net life output of the worker is a complicated subject where a number of balancing items have to be taken into account, and the final result is by no means obvious. We have to thank Dr. Lees[1] for clearing our minds on this subject and showing that perhaps the correct way of looking at this relation is that some countries spend more on health services because they are rich rather than that some countries are rich because they spend more on health services.

Here, then, is the dilemma. With these newer forms of public economic activity no balance can be struck with reasonable accuracy between the economic gains and losses following from changes in the scale of expenditure. The gross cost is known but not the net. To that degree the community is not certain what it is doing. And presumably the wider the area of public activity of this kind the greater the area of uncertainty. Where in these circumstances is the line of wisdom to be found? Of course, the search must continue for

[1] D. S. Lees, *Health Through Choice*. Institute of Economic Affairs, Hobart Paper 14.

novel and more precise forms of calculus and I shall have something to say about this in the following lecture. But what meanwhile? What if, even in the long run, the uncertainties cannot be resolved? If understanding of the society in which we live is prized highly, might it not be worth while paying a price for it, opting for one economic system which, even if it were less productive, at least seemed comprehensible as against another system which might or might not be more productive but which left us in a fog as to why the community had done one thing rather than another.

Pending any discoveries by which public expenditure could be decided upon more rationally, I would hazard, for the interim period, some simple precepts.

1. It is a cardinal principle of every free society that the State should possess, and use to the full, power to restrain the activities of one individual where it is patent that otherwise the liberties of others would be endangered. Such action, however, becomes progressively dubious as the infringement upon the liberty of the one becomes greater and the harm done to the many slighter and more debateable. For instance, it is one thing to insist that all members of the community shall have a basic minimum of education, since there can hardly be civilization without literacy. It is quite another to restrict choices in higher education on the

score that national economic necessity demands that a higher proportion of the able young should be steered into science or technology or management or languages or whatever aptitude is thought to be most critically lacking for the time being. For then a serious sacrifice is expected from the individual, that of being educated in terms of those subjects not spontaneously arousing his interests, whilst the diffused gains to the community are hypothetical, based as they are upon tenuous lines of reasoning.

2. It should not be overlooked that the very extension of public action with a given purpose may reduce the scale of private action to the same end. It is always the net result that should be searched for. State support for research by private firms may merely result in their cutting down what they themselves, in any case, intended to spend. Efforts by government to redistribute and equalize the existing endowments of higher educational institutions may diminish, for the future, private charitable contributions to education. A free National Health Service, paid for largely out of general taxation, not only discourages people from paying privately for their medical services but leads them to be content with a service of lower quality than they might otherwise have been prepared to pay for.[1]

[1] J. & S. Jewkes, *Value for Money in Medicine*. Blackwell, 1963.

3. Even though, in some cases, it is impossible to calculate exactly the economic returns likely to flow from the public provision of a service, yet it may often be reasonable to suppose that some forms of public provision are more likely to yield economic benefits than others, and should have prior claims on public resources. Thus in a National Health Service economic benefits are most likely to flow from preventive medicine, from medical services for the young, from capital investment in hospitals and medical schools and from medical research, particularly where the research is directed towards the cost of rendering medical services more cheaply.

4. Where public economic action can be shown to bring not only diffused advantage to the community as a whole but special discriminating benefits to individuals or groups, then it is always equitable and often expedient that the privileged individuals should make compensatory payments in one form or another. If, for instance, it is socially desirable to provide higher education for an able young man, because this will increase the national income, and if he can be expected to benefit more from this than anybody else, then he ought to pay for his own education (although he should be allowed to borrow from public or private agencies set up for the purpose). If he were not prepared to do this, it could only be because he rated

education so low as to call into question his right to privileges denied to other young people not so clever academically. So too with the public support of research and development on the part of a private firm in the ordinary commercial field. The firm is in as good, perhaps a better, position than any government to judge here. If it were not prepared to meet at least a part of the costs, this in itself would create the presumption that the firm does not believe that the work is commercially promising.

5. In some forms of public enterprise experimented with in Great Britain since the end of the Second World War, the rule has for the moment triumphed (not without some painful struggles to escape from the illusions of 'rational price structures') that the scale of any enterprise should in effect be determined by the test of the market, that the enterprise should go ahead as long as the prices it obtains are covering costs and as long as one part of the enterprise is not subsidizing another. But in other cases, especially health and education, the service has not been expected to cover its costs, the price system could not be used for distributing the necessarily limited supply, and some other method of rationing had inevitably to be adopted. The principle adumbrated was that 'need' must be met. But how can 'need' be determined? The answer usually is that it can be assessed professionally: the doctor can

decide what medical service a patient needs, the teacher what education an applicant needs. In fact, we know that there are no uniform professional standards. Different teachers would not agree as to whether a particular candidate could benefit from higher education; different doctors as to whether a particular course of treatment was necessary in a given case. But in both these professions it seems to be widely believed that the government is not meeting needs in total, that too little is being spent publicly on medicine or education. The possibility, therefore, cannot be ruled out that, in cases of this kind, where the government sets out to provide a kind of national charitable service, it may fail to make sufficient provision to meet aggregate needs, however defined, and thus expose each and every individual to the danger that his needs may not be met. It seems desirable, therefore, that there should always be an alternative channel of supply, that it should always be possible for the individual whose assessment of his own case differed from that of the government, to satisfy his need by making sacrifices in other directions. In brief, it may be that some form of pricing system would be of value here as it has been in the operation of the nationalized industries.

LECTURE THREE

Striking the Balance

If we ask what kind of economic institutions will best serve the purposes of the community, two points of departure immediately suggest themselves. One is to inquire: what have been the great failures and successes of public enterprise and private enterprise respectively in recent times? A second is to ask: what kind of an economic world do we in fact live in and what institutions are most likely to enable us to make the best of that environment?

I suppose there would be wide agreement that the outstandingly successful new function of government in our time has been the maintenance of full employment (although in some quarters of the United States the word Keynesian is still just as likely to cause a rush of blood to the head as the term *laissez-faire* in some quarters in Britain). It is proper to describe this addition to our economic knowledge, and the major policies which depend upon it, as revolutionary. Of course, the happy-go-lucky fashion in which governments have sometimes accepted this responsibility has brought its tribulations. The persistent inflation which has beset so many Western countries since the end of the Second World War is largely due, in my mind, to the attempts on the part of governments to force the rate of employment to heights which make inflation likely. Sometimes the efforts to supplement full employment policy by dealing with local pools of unemployment have started with the commendable purpose of encouraging mobility and minimizing the pains of adjustment but have finished with grandiose schemes for the control of the location of industry which may well have done more harm than good.

But, after all, there are times for counting blessings and one certainly is that massive unemployment of the kind from which the world suffered between the wars in the developed countries need not recur. This form of government intervention justifies itself on the critical counts. The government does for the individual what he cannot do for himself and it makes it less likely that the individual will find himself in a situation in which his instinctive actions to safeguard his interests will be self-frustrating or might even do him harm.

On the other hand, it seems to me that the recent efforts of governments positively to engineer economic growth have been among their most palpable failures. I must not be misunderstood here. Governments have the power, and indeed the responsibility, for creating an environment which will favour economic growth. They can reduce the pains of economic change and thereby weaken the irrational resistance to it. They can attack restrictive practices. They can lessen the loss arising from unused resources, especially of labour. But in recent years governments have gone far beyond all this in their efforts to improve standards of living. They have set up economic growth as a community aim transcending all others and they have gone through motions which would only have a meaning if they were, in fact, in possession of knowledge and techniques which gave them the power to determine, before the event, the rate of economic growth. Time is only too likely to dispel this illusion, as it did with the efforts of the British Government to plan the economic system between 1945 and 1950. In the meantime, however, harm may be done. Already this 'growthmanship' has led to some disillusionment and might easily lead to more, has injected confusion into public discussions of economic affairs and diverted attention from less spectacular, more painful but more reliable measures to improve standards of living.

I will illustrate from the history of central economic planning in Great Britain between 1962 and 1964, during the last two years of the Conservative Government and the early months of the Labour Government.

This planning centred on an annual average rate of growth in the economy of 4 per cent. The first obscurity was what exactly was meant by this figure. Was it an increase which it was thought would occur; or was hoped would occur; or was feared would not be achieved unless the Government engaged itself in these special measures? In the early days of 1962, the National Economic Development Council would go no further than to say that 'the implications' of a 4 per cent rate of growth should be studied.[1] Later it was stated by the Director-General of N.E.D.C. that 'Britain's economic policy is geared to a 4 per cent rate of growth'.[2] Clearly the choice of 4 per cent rather than some other figure cannot have been a wholly capricious act or the study of its implications a matter of idle curiosity. In fact, it came to be widely accepted that this rate of growth could be achieved and that the process of planning by the Government and N.E.D.C. would be a contributory factor to this end.

The choice of the figure 4 was, in one sense, surprising. It represented a rate of growth half as fast again as that which had occurred in the United Kingdom in the 1950's and twice as fast as the average for the first

[1] *Growth of the United Kingdom Economy to* 1966, p. viii.
[2] *Financial Times* Annual Review, 6th July 1964.

half of this century. The injection of some new impulse, powerful enough to modify long-established trends, was clearly being presupposed. And the only conceivable new factor in the situation was the inauguration of planning itself. This was described as 'revolutionary'.[1]

> This emphasis on growth—which involves basing economic policy on the dynamic concept of change—represents a major revolution in attitudes. It is a departure from the static approach represented by either the simple Micawber-type preoccupation with securing a satisfactory cash balance of income and expenditure or the more sophisticated Keynesian concern with the national balance of income and expenditure. In contrast the dynamic approach to economic issues looks to the future objectives of the economy, and the rates of growth needed to attain them.

The procedure as followed by N.E.D.C. became the more mysterious in that, apparently, it did not matter whether the plan was wrong or right. As the Director-General put it:[1]

> Deviations will occur and it does not reduce the value of forward assessments that market conditions may produce results different from those expected. An examination of the reasons for the difference between the result and the expectation can be of great value in helping to overcome difficulties.

[1] *Financial Times* Annual Review, 6th July 1964.

The forward assessments must either have had some influence or no influence on the action of people. If they had no influence, could there be any purpose in the plan? If they had some influence, would the existence of an incorrect forward assessment not have tended to lead people to behave in a wrong way and contributed to economic distortions?

In fact, the planned growth of 4 per cent was not achieved and when the Labour Government was formed in October 1964 the old plan was scrapped. But not before the divergence between the plan and reality had done harm in at least three ways.

1. The trade unions, understandably enough, came to think in terms of bigger annual wage increases than were consistent with the actual growth of the economy without creating inflationary pressure.

2. The impression that the economy was 'geared to' a 4 per cent rate of growth created a false sense of prosperity. Proposed increases in public expenditure were, therefore, less critically questioned than would otherwise have been the case. In the plan issued in 1962, N.E.D.C. put forward estimates of public expenditure for the period 1961 to 1966 showing percentage increases much greater than for the preceding period and greater than the actually achieved increase in economic growth.[1] By 1964 it was accepted on all

[1] *Growth of the United Kingdom Economy to* 1966, pp. 34–46.

hands that one cause of the economic difficulties of that year was excessive public expenditure. As the Labour Chancellor of the Exchequer said in the House of Commons on 8th December 1964:

> The great distress to me is to find that we have a growth rate of 2 per cent and programmes to which we are committed based on a growth rate of 4 per cent. This presents the whole House with a very real problem. . . .

3. Whilst the publication of the 1962 plan must have left the vast majority of those people who take the critical economic decisions, especially in the private sector, doing exactly what they would have done in any case, large public or semi-public institutions might well have based their programmes upon the unachieved national 4 per cent increase and thus been led into error and the misdirection of their resources. Thus the Central Electricity Generating Board based its expansion programme upon the 4 per cent figure 'in large measure as an act of faith'.[1] There is a wide margin between the concept of planning as a new, revolutionary and dynamic approach to the conscious manipulation of the economy and the ultimate resort to acts of faith in this way.

It is a reasonable assumption that the promulgation in 1962 of the 4 per cent figure contributed to the

[1] *Financial Times*, 30th November 1964.

economic difficulties which came to a head in the United Kingdom in 1964. Indeed, in the autumn of that year, sweeping criticisms were being made of it. The 4 per cent growth was variously described as a myth,[1] an incantation, a parrot cry. It might have been expected that, in consequence, the whole technique of planning in this form would have fallen into disrepute and that the State would have placed increasing emphasis upon measures to remove obstacles to growth, leaving the rate of growth to decide itself. This did not occur.

The new Labour Government allowed the old unfulfilled plan to lapse, thus (for those who attached importance to planning) leaving the country precariously naked of a plan. A new plan in outline was promised for the Spring of 1965 and in full detail for the Summer of that year.

Why then, despite these setbacks, did confidence in the principle of planning survive? One argument was that both the principle and the 4 per cent figure were sound but that the Conservative Government had failed to embody in its planning a factor to allow for its own incompetence and that another government would do better. Another was that the failure lay simply in the choice of a figure of 4 per cent and that

[1] A. Day, 'The Myth of Four Per Cent Growth'. *Westminster Bank Review*, November 1964.

a more careful examination of past trends and increased skill in prediction would produce a better figure, say 3½ per cent. Another was that, although the plan had failed in respect of the near period, nevertheless it could confidently be expected to produce the right answers for the long period; this based on the extraordinary belief that the distant future can be more clearly seen and understood than the immediate. Another was that the plan had not really failed, that the 4 per cent rate of increase had not been achieved but that it would ultimately be achieved; this is the argument that something can be performed 'but not in the time' which overlooks the point that, since time is of the essence, not to do something in the time amounts to not doing it.

But, at the time of writing (December 1964) the most ominous reaction of the failure of the plan was that planning might cease to be an effort in handling economic quantities in a rational fashion and progressively would become a weapon for political manœuvring. If one government has set a 4 per cent rate, even though that rate has not been achieved, will another government find it politically palatable to offer anything less? It was expressed thus:

> The figure of 4 per cent is now established in the public mind. . . . Over the next four or five years it will be fascinating to watch the confrontation between the

> political impossibility of stating a target of less than 4 per cent and the alleged economic impossibility of reaching it.[1]

This second period of experiment with economic planning in Britain since the end of the Second World War serves to confirm a conclusion which has been reached from other angles in the course of these lectures. The deeper a government involves itself in the working of the economic system, the more likely it is that, finding itself cornered, it will allow its so-called economic decisions to be vitally influenced by political expediency. This is not an atmosphere favourable to a self-understanding society.

Turning now to the other side of the shield, in what special ways has the strength or the weakness of private enterprise been revealed in recent years? The direct approach here would be to ask whether those countries which closely approximate to free economies have performed better than other countries, where *dirigiste* policies have been pursued. But I do not intend to follow that line. It is one on which if anything is said much would have to be said; where the literature is already vast and the conclusions arrived at by different authors conflicting or inconclusive. My feeling is that all such discussions should start out with

[1] F. T. Blackaby, '4 Per Cent Again'. *District Bank Review*, December 1964.

the challenging and undisputed fact that the United States has a much higher standard of living than other countries and to ask to what this can be attributed if not to private enterprise and free markets.

I prefer to use my limited time to put forward another, less usual, claim for private enterprise: that the free market is exercising a strong civilizing influence. This bald statement may at first sight surprise and even shock some people. It runs counter to conventional thought—which is that whilst capitalism has a great potential for getting stuff made, it is a way of producing wealth which constantly threatens to undermine our social and cultural standards. The curious may turn to one of the works of Sydney and Beatrice Webb, published in 1923, *The Decay of Capitalist Civilization*, to see how great, even pathological, has been the dread, in quite recent times, that economic competition must destroy the quality of our living. The Webbs claimed that capitalism would lead to the debasing of morals, the undermining of cultural standards, the wholesale adulteration of goods. But this is not the way the world has gone.

The profit incentive has, in fact, provided many of the material aids by which cultural standards have been raised and has done something, even under the most unpromising conditions, to force people into the habits of mutual tolerance. Let me illustrate. The most potent of all civilizing forces is the uncensored and easy access to the written word. Has anything in recent years done more to foster that than the appearance of the 'paperback', which has brought the larger part of human knowledge within the reach, at low cost, of virtually every interested person in the Western world? The paperback was devised and has been spread over great markets by men looking for private gain. The interest in great music has been stimulated in recent years by many inventions but especially by the long-playing record and refined devices for reproducing sound, which were invented in the laboratories of commercial firms and widely distributed by many firms in vigorous competition. The sense of form and colour has been fostered all over the world by the opportunity of amateur activity and experiment through the cheapening of the camera; the competition in the international market for cameras has in recent years gone on with a quite primitive gusto. Nearly all the chemical and mechanical devices by which in the last half-century it has become easier for the architect to employ new materials and forms, for the archaeologist to build up his knowledge of the past, for the librarian to store and provide a quicker access to the fund of existing knowledge, for the landscaper to create the patterns which match his wishes, have been the product of the inventiveness and skill in manufacture of men who were interested in personal profit. The argument (oddly enough, sometimes advanced by private businessmen anxious to defend a monopoly) that competition necessarily debases the quality of goods does not stand up to examination. There is no evidence of a general deterioration of consumers' goods in the Western world, or that the quality is rising least rapidly in countries where economic competition is most vigorous, or that within one country the competitive industries have a less satisfactory record than the monopolies, public or private.

One can, I think, go further and claim that within the model of the free market lies one good chance of smoothing the frictions which develop between men on the score of religion, race, colour or social values. 'The market is a great civilizer.' It is a rare kind of association: one in which the parties trade together voluntarily, do so only so long as they believe they are deriving benefits as producers or consumers and are always free to take their custom or their products elsewhere without creating grievances; one, that is to say, in which the game will only go on if both sides know they will win.

This simple but important idea is being advanced in these days by men in varying walks of life and of all political, social and economic views. Businessmen protest at trade boycotts, whether in respect of South Africa or of Cuba, of Spain or of China or Russia. They are, of course, concerned about their profits but they also point out, what is not easily refuted, that to stifle trade leaves all the problems still to be solved. Left-wing thinkers, anxious to narrow the gap between East and West, urgently call for more and freer commercial trading across that gulf. Right-wing thinkers invite us to ponder over the fact that 'racial discrimination has diminished earlier, faster and more quietly in the market-place than in political life'.[1]

Of course free markets are not going to provide any certain, simple and universal remedy for all the extraordinary tangles into which human beings manage to tie themselves. But it is true that wherever men, out of passion or intolerance, deliberately disrupt markets, then they damage their own economic interests. And the more widely that fact is recognized, the stronger will be the forces making for social tranquillity.

Of the flaws in private enterprise the one which seems to me most serious, which is awkward to handle and which, if it did continue and worsen, would be fatal to that system as a whole is monopoly. I summarize here the views which I have developed at length elsewhere.[2] There are strong forces tending to build up industrial monopolies. But there are other forces, and

[1] G. J. Stigler, *The Intellectual and the Market Place*, p. 88.

notably the process of technical change, which tend to break them down. What the final outcome of this struggle would be, in the absence of outside intervention, is a matter of doubt. Anyone who seriously advances the virtues of a competitive system should be prepared to put this matter beyond dispute by accepting the need for active intervention on the part of governments to exercise a watch over the industrial system for the purpose of discouraging monopoly. The effective public control of monopoly, however desirable it may appear, is not easy. Where monopoly arises through agreements between businessmen to control prices or output then there are, to my mind, well-tried ways of control which are adequate. The great problem, and one where it must be confessed the theory and practice of control is in something of a muddle in Western countries, is that of oligopoly, how far the size of a firm or the combined size of a group of firms should itself be regarded as inimical to the public interest irrespective of the market practices and performance of the firm or group. I see no reason why the problem should prove finally intractable. There is

[2] J. Jewkes, 'No Industry Without Enterprise'. *Rebirth of Britain*, p. 6. 'The Control of Industrial Monopoly'. *Three Banks Review*, December 1955. 'Monopoly and Economic Progress'. *Economica*, August 1953.

no evidence that over the last half-century competition has been declining or that 'competition contains the seeds of its own decay'. So there is no occasion to despair of ever finding working rules which will provide the benefits both of industrial competition and the economies associated with large-scale production.

I turn now to my second point of departure. What is the dominant feature of the world in which we live and, *a priori*, what kinds of economic institutions seem most likely to enable us to cope with it? It is undoubtedly *change*, change which is largely unpredictable. Let me hurry on to say that this is nothing new. Since the beginning of the Industrial Revolution it has always been true. I sometimes think that many of our present-day troubles are due to the habit of looking upon old problems as new and discarding well-tried methods of dealing with them in favour of unproved newer techniques.

It is impossible to portray fully enough to match the reality the totality of this change or to measure it adequately in figures. I will mention just one very recent instance which vividly illustrates the point. Less than a decade ago it was almost universally believed in Britain that the future lay with electricity for heat and power. Nearly everybody assumed that gas as a form of fuel was destined to die out altogether. Yet within the last year or two the picture has changed radically. From being one of the most technically stagnant industries the gas industry has jumped into the position of being one of the most exciting and promising. The use of coal in gas making is declining as a result of new discoveries. Costs are falling and promise to continue to do so. And other improvements seem to be in the offing.

If past experience is anything to go by we can take it for granted that the world will be one of shocks and surprises in which, far from being able to predict with confidence, we may be hard put to it to recognize promptly new situations even after they have developed. Here, then, is the dilemma. We cannot know the future but we cannot remain indifferent to it.

> True wisdom lies in the ability to mould one's life in accordance with the decrees of chance.

Here we come up against the critical difference of outlook from which so much controversy flows. The one group, 'the planners', regard man as fully fitted to be master of his economic destiny; they see no reason why he should ever be caught unawares; they feel that he should dedicate himself to the moulding and directing of the future in detail in accord with rational and humane principles. Different strategies have been favoured for harnessing change in this way. They range from what British governments call economic planning to what the Russian or Chinese governments call it.

The second group, 'the free market men', place emphasis on the need for unending adjustment to change, after it has occurred, through the spontaneous reactions of a market. They imply that a long series of small gradual changes will be preferable to infrequent large changes. They insist that 'a man never goes so far as when he does not know where he is going'.

The error into which the first group seem most likely to fall is that of attempting the impossible. The most likely mistake of the second group is that of devoting too little thought and imagination to the devising of new uses for the market and perhaps of advocating them too diffidently when they have been discovered.

The damage which is likely to follow when the impossible is attempted will be a function of the power possessed by those in control and their stubbornness in pursuing their aims. In the extreme case, when a government sets out to control from the centre all economic activity, success, of course, is unattainable. The government will then be tempted to seize new powers over the individual and, confronted still with the inevitable failures, will look for scapegoats—citizens who have not worked hard enough or have engaged in sabotage, or evil-intentioned foreigners.

Some of the greatest tyrannies have had their origin in the frustrations of those who have sought to do good by methods which were doomed to failure.

Where matters cannot be pushed to these limits, as in democratic Western countries, governments are likely to react to failure with further elaboration of their plans, and vast enterprises can finally be built up of a kind undreamt of at the outset. One striking illustration of this is found in the history of agricultural support in the United States.[1] Agriculture in America had been going through great changes and in 1929 the American Government set out to ease the pains of adjustment and to bring aid to the poorest farmers. Neither aim has in fact been achieved. The period of transition has been indefinitely prolonged and the benefits have probably gone much more to the well-to-do farmers. In the process the Government, step by step, has been drawn into new responsibilities and activities which have had their reactions upon nearly every facet of American economic policy, national and international, and has built up an empire of vested interests among those who operate and those who benefit from the schemes. The chain of events is well

[1] In this account I have drawn heavily on the writings of Professor Karl Brandt. See, in particular, his 'Growth of the Public Sector' in the symposium *The New Argument in Economics*, 1963.

known. The fixing of high farm prices produced large surpluses of agricultural products. The Government thereby became the owner of enormous stocks; it became responsible for their transportation by road and rail, their storage and rotation, their carriage abroad by rail and ship and often their transport within foreign countries. The presence of these huge stocks created new uncertainties in the market and destroyed all incentive for private stock holding. The efforts to dispose of a part of the stocks abroad led to intricate and not always happy relations with foreign countries and often rebounded to damage American industry, thus requiring further public compensatory measures. Attempts by the American Government to encourage larger economic trading regions in the world have been hampered by the obligations of the Government to insist upon the rights of the American farmer. This almost incredible, and still expanding, network of public activities has grown up unwittingly from the laudable intention of helping a comparatively small number of poor farmers.

Many other cases of the same kind, although on a smaller scale, could be cited. The British Groundnuts Scheme is certainly one and I suspect that our Atomic Energy Programme promises to be another.

Are there any practices or precepts which, if courageously adhered to, might enable a government to avoid this experience of taking one apparently innocuous or even commendable step and then of finding itself reluctantly and irresistibly drawn into follies it would have been glad to avoid? I think there are.

First, it would help if governments would define more exactly and pursue more directly what they want to do. In the last analysis many forms of government intervention are efforts to help poor people. Now if the aim is to deal with poverty why should not this be attacked directly? Why should poverty in a Western country not be got rid of by guaranteeing everybody a minimum income, through the use of a negative income tax or other device? Instead of this, governments tend to bring help to the old, although old people are not necessarily poor; or to the sick, although sick people may be well off; or to all farmers or some other group, although the members of that group may contain rich and poor. The result of all this has often been to create the most baffling inconsistencies. Rent subsidies in Britain made it impossible to determine exactly who was subsidizing whom, but it was certain that in many instances poorer people were being compelled to subsidize richer. With the National Health Service, depending so largely as it does on general taxation, it is quite conceivable that poorer people who happen to be healthy are subsidizing richer who are frequently sick.

A useful, perhaps an essential, supplement to the straightforward attack on poverty would be the public encouragement of personal insurance against the various vicissitudes of life. But, of course, we cannot expect the use of, and confidence in, insurance to increase unless the long-period value of money is maintained.

It would help, especially in cases where governments describe their new departures as experiments, if they would recognize that an experiment is not an experiment unless the possibility of failure is accepted and that to confess to failure, when it does occur, is not a sign of weakness but of strength. Why should face-saving have become such a highly developed form of political virtuosity? It might be possible to stipulate that all new forms of government intervention should have a specified term with a pre-determined rate of liquidation. If, for example, it were known from the outset that every new tariff had to be cut by 5 per cent per annum, it would reduce the demands for protection and make it easier for governments to do the courageous thing.

In the present position, in which there is much public intervention which many thinking people dislike but from which there appears to be no escape, perhaps first thoughts should go to possible stratagems by which these schemes could be gradually unwound and a return made to free market conditions. For example, under the present system of agricultural subsidies in many Western countries, farmers are earning a larger income or obtaining a higher price than they would obtain in the market. The subsidies, however, do not represent the total cost to the community. There is also the cost arising through the misallocation of resources. Much more important, there is the ever-widening circle of loss generated by the continuing defence of vested interests. Thus, the existence of a large and very highly subsidized body of German farmers greatly obstructed the work of creating a single economic entity within the Common Market. In such a situation, as in others such as rent subsidizing and tariff protection, it may often be worth while for the whole community, in order to get back to more rational economic arrangements, to grant once-for-all compensation to the vested interests.

There is little need to stress the inherent difficulties of getting governments to accept legislative or constitutional rules aimed at imposing long-period restrictions upon their own more prodigal or foolish habits. To many people there will be something repugnant in the idea of pensioning off those very groups who have longest been feather-bedded. But if the day ever arrives when governments do go directly for what they want; follow the straight road for its straightness; leave themselves opportunities for second thoughts and lines of retreat; disengage themselves from old unhappy obligations by boldly cutting losses; then I think the role of government would be looked at generally in a more open and rational way. For then the suspicions would be allayed both of those who now almost instinctively resist any new form of public activity as the thin end of the wedge and those who now can see only sinister motives in any doubt expressed about any extension of government functions.

So much for the trap into which the economic planners may fall of trying to do what cannot be done. What of the other group, those who put their trust in free markets, of whom I said a moment or two ago that they sometimes are slow to think out and recommend what is possible? Why has not more imagination been shown in exploiting the potentialities of the market process? I have already mentioned the deep-seated distaste that so many intellectuals of our age seem to have felt towards it and this must have had its influence. It is perhaps only to be expected that the proposal to introduce the pricing principle at some new point will normally arouse resistance because it endangers vested interests. Those who have most benefited from the pre-existing non-price methods of distribution may often be in a minority but they will be voluble in the defence of what they regard as their legitimate expectations. Those at whose expense these privileges have been provided will usually be a larger group who have felt the countervailing losses less keenly.

The use to which the pricing principle might be put in dealing with intractable economic and social problems, if only the traditional aversion to it can be removed and the resistance of vested interests overcome, can be illustrated through two very topical cases: the use of roads and the use of land.

Traffic congestion in most large towns has reached a point where social amenities are destroyed and economic efficiency seriously impaired. Perhaps nothing would bring greater and swifter relief than a system by which every driver of a vehicle, whether it was moving or parked, knew that he was incurring a charge directly related to his contribution to the congestion. He would then be under an inducement to make economical use of the roads and made aware of what his casual prodigality might be costing other people. So his private interest and his sense of social responsibility would both encourage him to act in such a way as would relieve the traffic pressure. And very many ingenious, and apparently quite practicable, methods of charging prices in this way are now available.[1]

This same principle appears just as attractive in the

[1] *Road Pricing: The Economic and Technical Possibilities*, Ministry of Transport, 1964.

handling of road shortages outside the towns as within them. There, it is easier to increase the supply of road services. The failure of successive British Governments since the end of the war to provide the country with a modern road system has been an error on a massive scale. If, since 1945, it had been possible, as in some other countries, for private institutions to build toll roads wherever they thought it possible to make profits, this supplementation of public action by private would have resulted in a better distribution of capital investment than has in fact occurred.

It may perhaps be protested here that what is being recommended is the adoption of a pricing system by public authorities and not by private enterprise. This is true, but it must not be overlooked that when public authorities do so act, the way is cleared for private enterprise also to come into play as a supplementary agent. For instance, so long as a public authority provides free parking on the limited road space in towns, commercial parking is less likely to be provided because private agencies must make a profit and must charge a price. The community is thus deprived of the thought and ingenuity that might otherwise have gone into the devising of more effective and economical methods of parking (multilateral parking and the like) most of which have been pioneered by private agencies.

The use of roads is a case where it has become evident that a shortage, brought about largely by rapid economic change, cannot be adequately remedied simply by the continuous increase of a free public supply. Under the duress of the facts, much thought is now being given to the use of pricing systems and private enterprise for escaping from the impasse.

In an equally important case, that of the use of land, thinking is still at so primitive a level and so charged with emotion that any suggestion that a more equitable and rational distribution of property rights could be brought about by the increased use of market processes tends to be received with incredulity or indignation.[1]

The first gap is that in information. There is no adequately organized market for the property in land, no comprehensive statistics, no constant contact between large groups of buyers and sellers. In the fog of ignorance, any statement, however extreme, will pass muster: that landlords are a small group of rich men interested only in exploiting the community; that most trading in land is speculation of an anti-social kind; that the deliberate holding of land from use is the underlying cause of the shortages and high prices of houses. From what limited knowledge exists all these

[1] See, in particular, the path-breaking work of D. R. Denman, *Land in the Market*. Institute of Economic Affairs, 1964.

charges are as incorrect as widely believed. The first stage in dealing with this unhealthy situation would be for the Government to encourage and aid in the creation of a more adequate market and the collection of the associated statistical and other information.

The second stage would be to apply simple economic logic in order to determine how far the forces of supply and demand could be relied upon to bring about defined ends, for what reasons and under what circumstances they might not work satisfactorily and with what confidence public intervention could be expected to improve on matters.

In some ways the market for land, of course, is not as other markets. Public authorities must possess the right to acquire compulsorily land for roads and other forms of communications; for the proper layout of towns and for the meeting of other urgent social needs where it can be shown that action by private interests is inconceivable. But it is a far cry from that to the suggestion that such land should be acquired below market price or that the acceptance of this particular sphere for public action is proof of the need for it over a wider area.

If land is in short supply in some places, as in the centre of cities, is it not desirable that the price should rise so that what there is should be put to the fullest and most economical use? It is not correct that the supply of land is fixed; every rise in price is a powerful inducement to extract greater benefits from it.

Speculation, especially through organized markets, such as the world commodity markets or the stock exchanges, is widely accepted as performing a useful function by smoothing out the course of prices and supplies, by operating as a flywheel in the world of commerce. Why should not land speculation bring similar benefits? If speculators take the risks of holding back land from some immediate and less valuable use for some long-distance and more valuable use and of systematically gathering together pieces of land so that they can be developed as a whole, and if the speculators stand to gain if their judgment be sound and society thereby benefits and to lose if they have fallen into error and society suffers, how does all this differ from the critical decisions and actions being taken by merchants and manufacturers every day the wide world over?

If land development and speculation leads to profits and if it is generally accepted that these should be taxed, why should they not be taxed in the same way as other gains instead of being struck at as if revenue-raising were very much a secondary consideration and the chastisement of sin the primary one?

And the other side of the medal should also be examined. There is no body of economic writings more shot through with fallacy than that, running from the works of Henry George down to the British Uthwatt Report, supporting the case for the wholesale or partial nationalization of the property in land. No public measures have led to more arbitrary confiscation of private rights or more complete frustration of their own declared purposes than those designed to give practical effect to the writings of land reformers. If something better is to be conceivable for the future, the onus is upon those who recommend wider public action in this sphere to show how it can be brought about.

To conclude. In these lectures I have sketched out my ideas on a wide canvas and devoted no less time to the asking of questions than to the providing of answers. This has been done deliberately, because in these days the vast majority of the growing army of economists see their task in quite different terms. With an utter absorption reminiscent of mechanics swarming over a racing car in preparation for the contest, they busily attend upon the economic system, each advocating with enthusiasm and confidence his own favourite nostrum for squeezing out of the system its last ounce of potential growth. The conception of the economic system as a kind of machine which can be directly, and relatively simply, manipulated by authority in order to maximize the wealth of the nation seems to me to be false and dangerous. The economic system is not a machine but an environment, a set of relations between human agents and natural forces, of such infinite and organic intricacy that we possess, and probably will continue to possess, only imperfect understanding of it. It is, therefore, not surprising that those who have challenged this view and have set out to make a man master of his economic destiny have left behind them a trail of economic wreckage, all the more melancholy because it was the outcome often of noble hopes and scientific pretensions. So that whilst it is necessary to record, line by line and chapter by chapter, the failures, it is just as apposite to stress that they were inevitable.

Those who believe that the best chance of inducing economic growth lies in creating the most favourable economic environment and then leaving things to grow, recognize that the results will nearly always be unexpected in one way or another. This prescription for success is much vaguer than the other but, judged by experience, it seems more likely to do good and less likely to do harm. The essence of it can be stated thus: that economic system is most likely to grow in which new ideas are given full and impartial scrutiny; new organizations are not crushed by vested interests; novelty and the questioning of accepted ways are stimulated; frequent and spontaneous adjustment to change are always possible and finality in any set of arrangements unthinkable.

So that if we turn to the nagging enigma, how far do the size and form of institutions influence their effectiveness in action, it is the *ecology* of the matter that counts; it is the right range, the right combination of sizes and forms which should be sought for. When, for instance, the efficiency of an industry is under examination, the presence of different products, technical processes and market conditions, varying aptitudes among businessmen, all lead to the presumption that there is not one size of firm which constitutes the optimum but a range of sizes among firms which will provide the highest efficiency in the industry. If one turns to the study of the rate of innovation and how that is connected with the different ways in which research is carried on, the virtues of eclecticism again become evident. The circumstances under which modern inventions have arisen are so diverse that, for the future, safety would appear to lie in numbers and variety of attack. New discoveries spring up at practically any point, any time and under any set of circumstances. The only real danger would seem to be in plumping for one method, one type of research institution, one source of new ideas to the exclusion of all others.

And so with this present topic: Public and Private

Enterprise. If it could be taken for granted that neither the one nor the other would be allowed to claim or acquire exclusive rights of operation except in the very limited number of cases where there was virtual unanimity as to the need for it. If in those special instances the watch over monopoly was constant, vigilant and even suspicious. If as much thought and interest could be directed to the fuller uses of the potentialities of the market system as to the possibilities of using public powers more extensively. If more thought could be given to those situations where a symbiosis of public and private enterprise appeared to open up promising fields. If, in those cases where direct competition between public and private enterprise promises to be fruitful, we could design ways of guaranteeing 'fair competition' between the two, a design which would rule out neither the possible bankruptcy of the private institution nor retrenchment or closing down of public enterprises not showing a surplus. If, both in the case of public and private enterprise, it were always kept in mind that, after a certain point, every new additional task threatens the efficiency with which present tasks are being performed. If it were recognized that spontaneous organizations, of which the market is one outstanding example, can expand without piling up administrative complexities as do conscious organizations. If all these things came to pass then we would have increased our chances of enjoying an economic system, at once more rational and productive, whose day-to-day performance would no longer need to be brooded upon, as at present, with neurotic trepidation.

INDEX